I0821746

Natural Resources

AIR

Christopher Forest

DiscoverRoo
An Imprint of Pop!
popbooksonline.com

abdobooks.com

Published by Pop!, a division of ABDO, PO Box 398166, Minneapolis, Minnesota 55439.

Printed in the United States of America, North Mankato, Minnesota.

102019
012020

THIS BOOK CONTAINS RECYCLED MATERIALS

Cover Photo: iStockphoto
Interior Photos: iStockphoto, 1, 5, 6–7, 10, 13, 15, 16, 23, 29 (top), 29 (bottom); Shutterstock Images, 9, 11, 17, 18–19, 20–21, 24–25, 26–27, 28, 30, 31; ALMA (ESO/NAOJ/NRAO)/ European Southern Observatory/Science Source, 12

Editor: Sophie Geister-Jones
Series Designer: Jake Slavik

Library of Congress Control Number: 2019942473

Publisher's Cataloging-in-Publication Data

Names: Forest, Christopher, author.

Title: Air / by Christopher Forest

Description: Minneapolis, Minnesota : Pop!, 2020 | Series: Natural resources | Includes online resources and index.

Identifiers: ISBN 9781532165832 (lib. bdg.) | ISBN 9781532167157 (ebook)

Subjects: LCSH: Air--Juvenile literature. | Air quality--Juvenile literature. | Natural resources--Juvenile literature. | Environment--Juvenile literature. | Ecology--Juvenile literature.

Classification: DDC 533.6--dc23

WELCOME TO DiscoverRoo!

Pop open this book and you'll find QR codes loaded with information, so you can learn even more!

Scan this code* and others like it while you read, or visit the website below to make this book pop!

popbooksonline.com/air

*Scanning QR codes requires a web-enabled smart device with a QR code reader app and a camera.

TABLE OF CONTENTS

CHAPTER 1

A CLEAR SKY

A family hikes on a mountain trail. The sky is bright and blue. The hikers stop for a break and breathe deeply. The air is fresh and clean. Fluffy white clouds drift high above.

WATCH A VIDEO HERE!

As people climb higher above sea level, the air they breathe contains less oxygen.

Air is a mix of **gases**. These gases are invisible. But they make it possible for life to exist on Earth. Carbon dioxide and oxygen are two gases found in air.

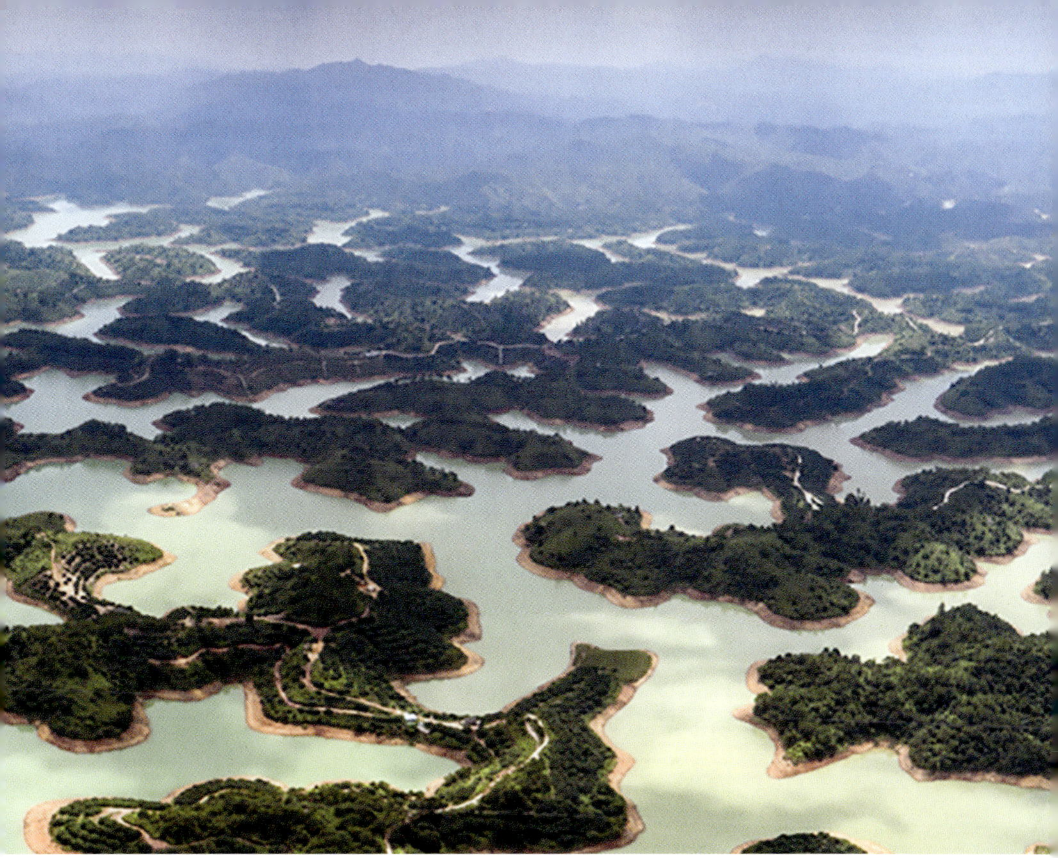

Plants take in carbon dioxide and release oxygen in a process called photosynthesis.

Plants need carbon dioxide to grow.

Animals need oxygen to breathe.

DID YOU KNOW?

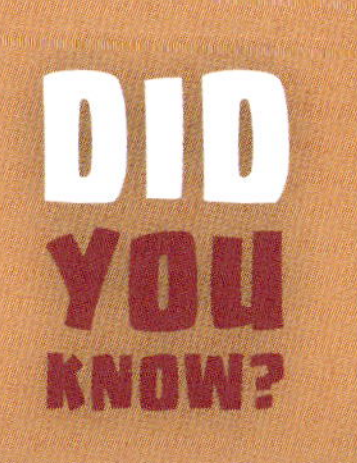

Air is mostly made up of a gas called nitrogen. Approximately 78 percent of the air is nitrogen.

CHAPTER 2

AN AMAZING ATMOSPHERE

Air forms layers around Earth. Each layer is a different thickness. Together, these layers make up the **atmosphere**. The atmosphere surrounds and protects the planet.

COMPLETE AN ACTIVITY HERE!

ATMOSPHERE LAYERS

The atmosphere has five main layers. Some layers contain a gas called ozone. Ozone stops radiation from reaching Earth. Radiation is energy that comes from the sun's rays. It can cause sunburns, and it can harm plants and animals.

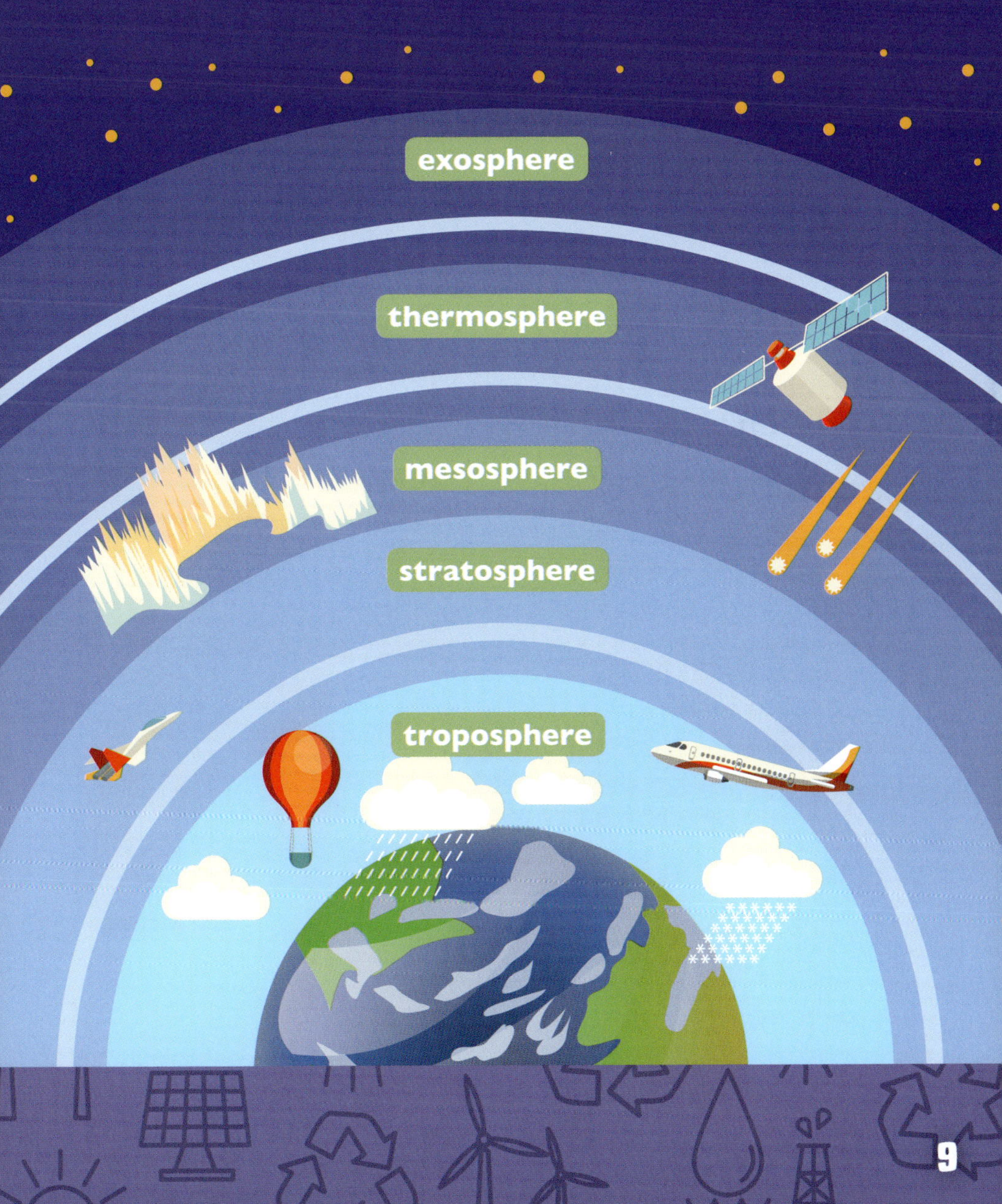

The **gases** in the atmosphere trap energy from the sun. They keep the planet warm enough to support life. Without these layers of air, the planet would be too cold for plants and animals.

Mars has a very thin atmosphere. As a result, the planet's average temperature is −81 degrees Fahrenheit (−63°C).

Earth's atmosphere protects the planet from the extreme cold of outer space.

DID YOU KNOW?

Earth's atmosphere is 300 miles (483 km) thick!

Changes in air pressure can cause bottles to collapse.

Air is invisible, but it still has weight. **Gravity** pulls the air toward Earth. The weight of the air pushes down on Earth's surface. This force is called air pressure.

Changes in air pressure can cause storms to form.

CHAPTER 3

POLLUTION

Sometimes harmful particles or **gases** enter the air. These particles or gases are called air pollution. Natural events are sometimes the cause. For example, wildfires and volcanoes can send smoke

LEARN MORE HERE!

Smoke from a wildfire can affect air up to 100 miles (161 km) from the actual fire.

and ash into the air. However, humans cause most air pollution.

Humans create pollution in many ways. Many factories and power plants burn **fossil fuels** for power. Their huge smokestacks release gases into the air. Cars create lots of **exhaust**.

Smoke from power plants often contains harmful chemicals.

The chemicals in acid rain can pull important nutrients from plants.

ACID RAIN

Dangerous gases in the air sometimes combine with **water vapor** in clouds. Such mixing causes acid to form in the water vapor. This mixture can fall to the ground as acid rain. Acid rain contains higher levels of acid than normal rainwater. Acid rain pollutes the water and land it touches. It also harms plants and fish.

And people release harmful chemicals when they burn trash.

Too much air pollution can form a thick layer near the ground. This is called smog. Smog can make it hard for people to breathe. Some people have to stay indoors when smog surrounds a city. Smog can hurt people's lungs and hearts.

In 2018, China build a 328 foot (100 m) tall tower that fights pollution and cleans the air.

Some cities have so much smog that it is unsafe for people to go outdoors.

Pollution can also damage Earth's **atmosphere**. Humans release chemicals into the air. These chemicals cannot escape the atmosphere. They are

As Earth's average temperature increases, some areas experience heavier rainfall and more flooding.

called greenhouse gases. The increase of greenhouse gases causes climate change. Humans, animals, and plants all add greenhouse gases to the atmosphere.

CHAPTER 4

MAKING CHANGES

Scientists are looking for ways to reduce air pollution. Many are looking for cleaner sources of energy. Wind and water create clean energies. People are working together to keep the air clean.

LEARN MORE HERE!

Trees absorb carbon dioxide. Planting them can help fight air pollution.

The countries that belong to the United Nations are creating rules to prevent air pollution. These laws limit the harmful **gases** released by vehicles.

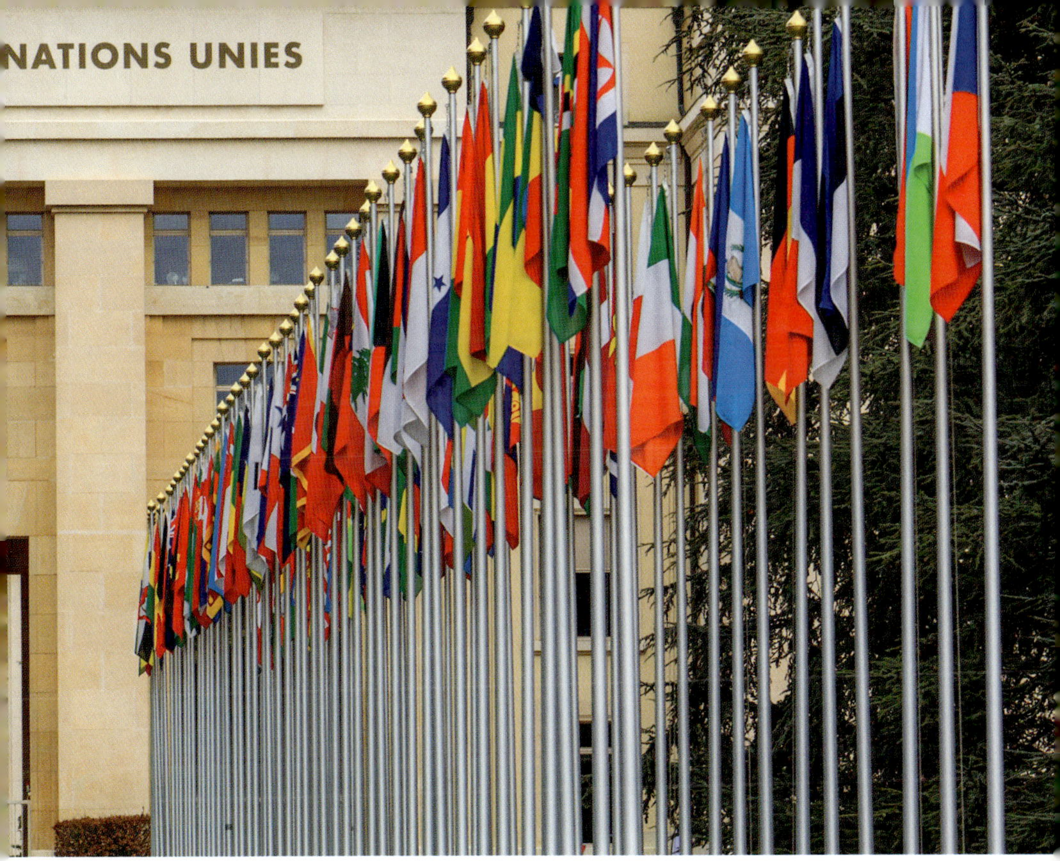

The United Nations was formed in 1945 to help countries around the world work together.

This helps prevent carbon dioxide from building up in the **atmosphere**.

DID YOU KNOW?

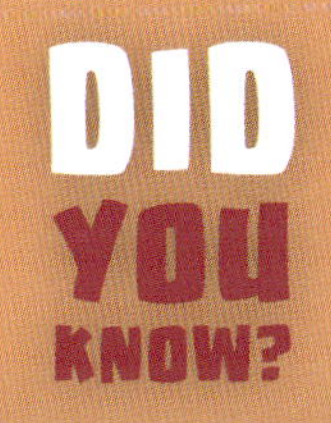

Carbon dioxide is the most common greenhouse gas. Fire can produce carbon dioxide.

Families can fight air pollution too. People can walk or bike instead of driving. That way, they will create less **exhaust**. People can also limit their use of electricity. For example, families

By biking instead of riding in cars, families can help keep the air clean.

can turn off lights and appliances when not using them. These objects run on electricity. Electricity is often made by burning **fossil fuels**. By using less, people can help protect the planet.

REDUCING POLLUTION

1963

Clean Air Act of 1963: The United States begins its first program designed to control air pollution.

1970

Clean Air Act of 1970: Another law aims to reduce air pollution in the United States by reducing pollution coming from vehicles.

1987

Montreal Protocol on Substances That Deplete the Ozone Layer: 197 countries around the world agree to stop using chemicals that reduce the ozone in the air.

1997

Kyoto Protocol:

Many countries agree to limit greenhouse gas emissions. The agreement has mixed results.

2015

Paris Agreement:

Countries make another attempt to reduce greenhouse gas emissions and control climate change.

MAKING CONNECTIONS

TEXT-TO-SELF

Have you ever seen smoke, smog, or other forms of air pollution? If so, where were you?

TEXT-TO-TEXT

Have you read other books that mentioned pollution? What ways of reducing pollution did those books describe?

TEXT-TO-WORLD

Air is just one natural resource that is affected by pollution. What are other resources near your home that could be affected by pollution?

GLOSSARY

atmosphere – the layers of gases that surround a planet.

exhaust – smoky waste from cars, power plants, or other engines.

fossil fuel – fuel made from the remains of plants and animals that died millions of years ago.

gas – a state of matter that does not have a shape and moves easily.

gravity – a force that pulls together any objects with mass.

water vapor – water in the form of a gas.

INDEX

ONLINE RESOURCES

popbooksonline.com

Scan this code* and others like it while you read, or visit the website below to make this book pop!

popbooksonline.com/air

*Scanning QR codes requires a web-enabled smart device with a QR code reader app and a camera.